Your Legacy
MOMENT

Your Legacy MOMENT

Published by Krystal Lee Enterprises (KLE Publishing)
Copyright © 2025 by K. Lee All rights reserved. Please
send comments and questions:

Krystal Lee Enterprises
770-240-0089 Ext. 1
sales@KLEPub.com

To Reach the Author:
Email: me@authorklee.com or me@drkrystallee.com

Web: www.AuthorKLee.com
Social Handle: AuthorKLee on all pages
FB, IG, Tiktok, Twitter (X), Pinterest, LinkedIn, YouTube

ISBN: 978-1-945066-91-7

DEDICATION

I dedicate this book to communities that have been suffering and are in need of change. We start to change the world around us as we begin to change within ourselves.

My goal is to empower 1 million families to have access to resources that will help them preserve their legacy, build businesses and wealth, but also encourage them to live for the days they have.

When you leave this earth, it is my heart's desire that day will be a day filled with positively charged emotions, videos, books, pictures, words, and audios that keep your heart and purpose alive for all the years to come.

Thank you to my village, my support, children, family, and friends. Thank you to those who are willing to share free resources, allowing us to bless families with over $5,000 in complimentary gifts! To my Lord and Savior, thank you for giving me the vision to create Your Legacy Moment and all it will do to help families.

To you, the reader, thank you for taking the time to read and share this book. I trust it will bless you and your family for many years to come!

Your Legacy MOMENT

Table of Contents

Introduction
YOUR LEGACY MOMENT

I know it might be scary to think about life after you leave earth. Just reading this sentence can stop our breath, can't it? I am not writing this book to scare you into decisions or guilt-trip you into buying or doing something. This book is for those who care about their future and those they love–but also about your here and now.

This book is a labor of love, and I believe that those who love themselves, their children, or the family members in their life, whether through blood or circumstance, want their family not to be burdened by their passing, but to see it as a time for rejoicing. It can be hard to rejoice when someone passes when you know their life was not secure. When you know they left a lot of loose hairs, that will become moments of argument, legal battles, debt, frustration, or continued pain for others.

Nothing is worse than having a key you die with in your hands. Your children, grandchildren, and those whose lives you impact need your story in the same way they had required your presence. If you think for a second that your life doesn't matter, I want to assure you, like an African proverb records, "We stand on the shoulders of our ancestors." No, not every ancestor is your blood relative. Still, I am sure we can agree that we all benefit from the life's work of people like Martin Luther King, Malcolm X, George Washington Carver, Harriet Tubman, Alexander Miles, Thomas Jennings– and I am about to mess you up by saying this. The Lord Himself, Jesus aka Yashua the Christ!

Yes, what would we all do if his life weren't recorded? If people who thought they were nobody chose to do nothing to preserve the greatest works the Father did in their lives? A people who were the least, the Father performed miracle after miracle to carry them through the darkest hours. How would we know where we come from if the victors of our wars were the only ones telling the stories?

We would have false narratives about who we are, who we were meant to be, and how life was for us. We would miss out on the key points that will touch the soul and help us to reach further into our bloodline. We would lose our grip and sight of the future because we have not appreciated the journey forward.

To create a strong family, you need a strong foundation to build upon. I know, many of us came from families who had no books recording our history. Who had one family member who kept everything, and when they died, those pictures ended up in the trash. We have family members who avoid family reunions like the plague!

We come from families that are trying to cope with their own pain and problems, and thinking of others can be a challenge. We have to become a gentle or a harsh reminder that if we don't value each other, how then will we learn to value those outside our family and across the street? We have to see the value in everyone because it will create a level, a standard, that will push us all to be and do better. When you realize you have a rich and strong legacy, dignity can be given back to you.

I want to encourage you right now that where you are, how you feel, and what you are going through, it all matters! I want to show you, through these five sections in this book, how you can do a life overhaul starting right where you are. We cannot live in reverse; we must live moving forward. I want to encourage you to care about the body you have and the soul that will always live on.

This is not a book that will dive heavily into concepts, but it is meant to show you powerful principles that will help you build a legacy that you and your family can stand on long after you are gone. This is the power of a legacy; it will never die. Your story will forever be told in words, video, and impactful stories through those you choose to invest in. Your investments are time, energy, money, resources, care, and having a heart to serve.

Turn the pages in this short and powerful book that will impact your life!

Emotional Health
SPIRITUAL AND EMOTIONAL HEALTH

I begin at the point in life that I find to be the anchor for my life. I know this is the part of life that many of us can either take for granted or postpone to the seconds before we die. I encourage you not to do that. I have been to funerals for people of all ages and walks of life. People who have been faithful, and many who have not been, to God or anyone else. We might think that because we are doing "okay," we don't have to change anything to secure our spiritual future.

We have all heard the jokes and been a part of conversations where choosing someone to preside over a funeral can be tough based on how people lived their lives. We wonder, where are they going if they were mean, rude, lawbreakers, cheaters, and deceivers? The truth is that we know the judgment of sin. But for those who may not know, have never heard it said, when we leave this life, how we lived here on earth will matter for how we spend our eternity.

Whether you spend your time with God, Yah, the Father, or you are separated from His face, that is where you will remain if He doesn't have mercy on your soul. Your soul is carried by the body you walk in, live in, and move around in. This body is important, and in the pages to follow, I will talk more about how to care for it out of love. Sometimes we know to do something, but we don't because of too many obstacles. I believe when the cares of this life weigh us down, we can miss protecting our peace here on earth!

Some may not want to talk about heaven or hell because the concept scares them. To think you will be in hell forever with no chance at having a second chance seems harsh. How can an all-loving God want me to be in hell all of my life? We may think, surely I have suffered enough, why should I suffer even more in the afterlife? One key concept you have to see in this series of questions is the me factor. When we make ourselves the center of our existence, everything is based off of us, our feelings, wants, desires, hopes, and dreams.

With a me-centered life, you don't leave room for anyone, including God. Can you imagine this: you got a friend, because we know you are not the one who fits this situation. You have a friend who doesn't invite you to any events, doesn't call, won't show up for you, won't text, write, or send a letter to you. They have never sat down for a meal with you or participated in anything that you wanted them to do. Would you invite this person to your wedding?

I know, you might invite them to a small party, or don't care if they come in unannounced, but your wedding is for what? Family and close friends. You aren't worried about your fifth cousin removed? With the Father, His ways are higher than ours. What more do you think He expects of us, in closeness, than we give Him? To sit at His table, be in His presence, to touch the hand and face of God, how much do you think you need to sacrifice to live in paradise?

Paradise is not about golden streets and mansions–although that is there, it is the Presence of Yahweh, the Creator of all things, and all who believe will be reunited with Him. He will walk among us in the coolness of the day like before. He is the One, and only one redeeming His creation and returning us back to His master plan. We can get mad at the game, we can hate the circumstances, but the earth you were born on, you cannot change it. We cannot change it.

The rules He set in place, I think we need to understand, were for your protection. He gives us wisdom and good things because it is His intention to bless you as your soul prospers. As you seek His Face, He says that He will be indebted to no man and whatever you gave Him, here on earth, He will give back to you today and in the future. So why are many of us not focusing on what matters here on earth? Why are we careless with our bodies, family, social structures, emotional well-being, mental health, and financial strength?

When we realize that we are building a legacy not just for earth, but also for wherever our soul will live, our seed of life will go, and we must realize we are as deep and our roots as wide as tree branches. The tree is such a good depiction of family, because strong leaders build branches that birds can come and find shelter in. When we protect our lives and train up our children in the way that they should go, when they are old, they won't depart from knowing the way!

This scripture doesn't mean they won't make mistakes, that they won't get on our nerves, or even spend time lost in the wilderness. We pray they don't die in their wilderness, but if we are being real, it happens every day. Eli's sons died in their wilderness, in trespasses and sins. His judgment for not correcting his boys was a limitation on the number of years and financial stability his legacy would have; our choices impact our children and shape the future.

Yes, it sounds unfair to be negatively affected by the works of others. But think about all the good we could do and leave to our children if only we saw the value in looking out for them. If we spend this time building up a life for ourselves, our children, and the world around us, how large would your tree grow to become? Do you care how large your legacy becomes or who knows it?

I would hope so because the world, your family, needs you, and if not, they should want you. When you are doing great, who doesn't want to claim your name? Who doesn't want to say watching you succeed, that is my cousin, sister, brother, mom, family member, or friend. Some are even content with saying they knew you when they were growing up. How did you impact their lives, though?

It is sad that some will take advantage of what you

taught them and never come back to thank you. But our God in heaven will reward your good deeds. He will bring honor where others thought to steal it away from you. The truth is still coming out from the many inventions stolen by white slave owners back nearly 200 years ago. The lives of those important to your history are being unearthed, and we are learning a deeper truth about our existence because of the seeds of the righteous.

I know it is not always easy to be the seed of the righteous. To do right, when you see or feel that everyone around you is doing wrong. I want to encourage you that no one should be able to distract you from the love of God. He is so loving that He redeemed all humanity, but He does require a response from you. Not a payment that you cannot afford. He wants you to love Him. Love endures all things. Love is patient, kind, and long-suffering. When He calls home a loved one, who you thought should be here, we have to be long-suffering and pray through our own emotions.

When He tells us "no" and we were hoping for a "yes," we have to be patient and not take out our frustrations on other people. We have to be open to His direction and protection. He knows the plans He has for you, "plans to prosper you and not to harm you, plans to give you hope and a future. Jeremiah said it correctly, the Father wants you to want what is best for you, because our selfishness will have us come up empty. We will be empty. We will harm ourselves, and our souls will suffer.

I want this section dedicated to your soul to challenge you to ask a few simple questions. This will help you to take an assessment of where you are and where you hope to belong. I know on this earth, one thing is hard to do: find a place to belong. For many of us, we find comfort in people who are like us. People who may look, sound, act, or think like us. But what if these environments are toxic? What do you do?

What if the way you have learned to survive is beneath what the Father has for you? What if you have determined in your heart that you deserve hell and don't mind going if you can have what you want today? Some are trading their time, children, future, health, and life for things, people, relationships, jobs, careers, or businesses. None of these things will feel worth it when you realize all it robs you of.

The busy parent who never spent time investing in their children. Although they have a series of actions they have done, what we don't do out of the right heart is just money spent, and activities we do to keep busy. It will get burned up in the fire of judgment. Don't you know in this life, you have to make an account for how you live your life? How you treated your parents and children. What you do for the least, the Father said you did for Me.

What have you done for others lately? What have you done for yourself to help you build a healthy relationship with God? I want to encourage you that if you are not saved, and are unsure of the afterlife, if you are not a child of God, or you don't belong in the Kingdom of God. The Kingdom of God does not start in heaven; it begins here on earth. "Thy Kingdom come, your will be done, on earth, as it is in heaven." The time to organize your soul, that is your mind, will, and emotions to serve God, is now.

Not when you die. Not only when you cry. Not just when life is tough, but every day we are to practice love. God is love, have you ever heard that? If you are heart-broken right now, I want to tell you He cares about that. If someone scared you off from the church, a building that made you think leaving them meant you had to leave God, I want to encourage you to turn back around again. Those people have no heaven or hell to put you in.

The One who has the power to put your whole body in hell is the One you ought to fear. Men, what can they do but talk? They talked about the Messiah, too! They hoped that their discouragement and threats would make Him stop His assignment on earth. They may be praying for you to abandon your post in God, and for you to give in to the seed of rebellion. But don't; you know that rebellion is like witchcraft? It is written in the Bible that when we rebel against the knowledge and wisdom of God, we are operating in witchcraft!

Some churches, people, circumstances, thoughts, or ideas you have to be willing to leave behind you. Not all things done under the sun glorify God. The devil knows the word, and his art is to make his actions appear as if they come from an angel of light. It might sound good for a moment to ignore people. To shut off

17

God, because we think we are hurting Him when He hurts us. Or at least, we believe He hurt us by taking a family member, keeping a husband or wife from us, because He didn't save someone in a way we expected.

But who is God? Who knows all things? Who knows where the thunder is held? Who knows where the leviathan is, a dragon, but God? But you, us, we think that we know best, and shake our fist at God. My mom told me the story of Dracula once. I never watched the movie; I'm not into horror movies at all, including vampire and werewolf movies. So, somehow we got on this conversation and she said, "The real Dracula wasn't a practicing witch. He was a believer, a Christian who got mad that God allowed his wife to die."

In his bitterness of soul, he cursed God and said he wouldn't serve him anymore. He grew ill over several months, and nothing seemed to cure his sickness. Instead of him repenting, he kept on cursing God, and so he needed a blood transfusion to survive. He had all the money, but no amount could save his soul from the emotional hell he was in.

They kept giving him blood from animals, until one day it wasn't enough. At this moment, he turned his need for blood from animals and decided to feast on people. Then miraculously, his teeth grew longer, and that was all she wrote! When my mom told me the story, I could see how we do that, too. How we can become a monster by allowing something to eat us alive inside, and tear us up emotionally. We can turn on the very people sent and were helping us.

Those with dementia and memory loss no longer recognize their loved ones. It can be gutwrenching for someone you love so much to forget you. Some who lose their memories can grow to dislike and even hate their family members. Those who broke your heart, abandoned you, or left you for dead. Those who might as well sucked the life out of you because after them, you were a shadow, a ghost of your former self.

Faithful Heart
ACCESS THIS BOOK

I want to encourage you. There is a verse in the bible that asks the question, "Can these dead bones live again?" It is a worthy question because many of us don't feel alive. We feel like the walking dead. We are surviving, but we have no peace if we are honest. We try to find it in food, family, money, sex, drugs, alcohol, or whatever else we indulge in. We soon discover that these highs wear off, and we remain stuck in the same spot. They don't move us from where we are to somewhere else; they only close our eyes as we walk in the same place for months, years, or even decades.

If you are tired of being in a padded room that is your life, emotional healing is necessary. Yes, forgiveness is part of the equation, but salvation is the first step. How can you forgive someone when you have not healed? How can you heal if you don't have the strength? How can you work and do what you need to do when you are depressed, living in a world with drawn curtains, dancing in the darkness with music blasting, or watching tv being rocked to sleep by the voices? How can you become bold when you are fearful?

Perfect love cast out fear! Love is what the Father wants to give you to cast out all unrighteousness. He wants you to practice love with Him, so He can strengthen you to pour Him out on all others you meet and see. He wants you to be a vessel of honor in His hands. We are of common use when we don't serve the Lord. When we are against the Kingdom of God, we are a vessel of dishonor, the Bible says. You don't have to live like this when saving grace is here to pull you out.

If you want out, I want to invite you to explore the salvation road with me. I want to encourage you to look at your life and ask the question: "Do I need to be saved?" Not only do I need to say words I feel in my heart. Our emotions can mislead us, but your sincerity is in your actions that follow this prayer. It is in the thoughts you have, the intentions, and the hope you have.

During the prayer of salvation, you want to ask for forgiveness of your sins, but it is important to know what sins you have committed in asking for forgiveness. To repent means to turn away from what you did before, and choose to follow the direction of the Word, the bible instead. There are many other sins that are spoken about in Galatians 5:19, that you also want to stop doing, so you don't miss the Kingdom of God.

Verse: "Now the works of the flesh are evident: sexual immorality, impurity, sensuality, 20 idolatry, sorcery, enmity, strife, jealousy, fits of anger, rivalries, dissensions, divisions, 21 envy, drunkenness (high or lacking sobriety), orgies, and things like these. I warn you, as I warned you before, that those who do such things will not inherit the Kingdom of God."

The salvation prayer is an experience and not a checklist. It is a commitment and one that should not be taken lightly. This is a prayer that will commit your life to be subject to the rulership of the Word of God, and anything that rises up against the Word of Truth, you must condemn through love (2 Corinthians 10:5). This scripture reads, "We destroy arguments and every lofty opinion raised against the knowledge of God, and take every thought captive to obey Christ."

You will become a new creature, and the old things will pass away (2 Corinthians 5:17). And this scripture reads, "Therefore, if anyone is in Christ, he is a new creation. The old has passed away; behold, the new has come." This prayer is life-transforming, and you will go through an experience. Some will love the change Yashua (Jesus) will bring to your life, and others will not like it, because sadly, they too don't like the Word of God.

I want you to know that this is okay. Don't be afraid. Don't stop your journey if you are rejected by family, friends, or others you care about. You have a family that is here for you, and this is the Body of Christ

(1 Corinthians 12:12-27), the unit that is the Church (1 Corinthians 12:27). You become a Child of God because you believe and love God and are now called by His Name.

I know this is a lot, so I encourage you to find a home church that is filled with the power, the Spirit, and the Love of God to disciple you and help you grow. This book will help you to pray and welcome your Lord and Savior to areas of your life that need transformation. This is the start of your road, but it will be glorious because Yah will complete the great work He started in you (Philippians 1:6). So don't worry about what you look like today, know that God is bigger than it all and can redeem you.

This verse reads, "And I am sure of this, that he who began a good work in you will bring it to completion at the day of Jesus Christ." Another good verse you must know is Deuteronomy 31:8, "It is the Lord who goes before you. He will be with you; he will not leave you or forsake you. Do not fear or be dismayed."

Alright, if you are ready to change your life and welcome THE God of all creation to enter your life through the Word of God, His Son, who died on the cross to pay for the sins of the world, who was given as a gift from Yahweh to reconnect us to Him after the fall of Adam, I invite you to walk with me through the prayer of salvation.

"Father, I thank you for impressing your truth on

the heart of "Say Your Name." I thank you for allowing one who was lost to become found today, and in
this moment."

Now, repeat after me.

"Father, I come to you because I need you. I need
you to save me from the mistakes I made and the sins
I have committed against You. I ask that you forgive
me for the sins that I have: (list your sins). Show me
the right way to live my life. I confess that Yashua/Je-
sus is the Son of God, that He died on the cross for my
sins, rose from the dead, and sits at the Right Hand
of the Father. I ask you to come into my life to be my
Lord and Savior. I thank you for making me a new
creation, in   Yashua's/Jesus's name, Hallelujah, and
so be it!"

You have made a tremendous commitment, and I
want to give you some helpful free resources. I want to
invite you to come on Mondays at 7:30pm EST to my
online book club, where we will help you see how to live
this life and connect with other believers. The books
we featured are God inspired, but they are real stories
about men and women, and how God can redeem anyone.

The second gift I want to give you is a 7-Day Journey from the "Bless the Works of My Hands a 21-Day
Devotional and Journal" book. This weekly excerpt will
help you start the journey to incorporate daily prayer,
devotionals, or bible readings into your schedule. This

will include a video and text message reminders for each of the 7 days. If you like the experience, I encourage you to upgrade the offer and complete the remaining 14 days.

Book Club & 7-Day Journey
ACCESS THIS FREE RESOURCE

Let's continue this casual conversation for the steps to preserve your legacy.

Mental Health
THERAPY, COUNSELING, AND
MENTAL HEALTH

Okay, I know that salvation feels good and looks good on you, but what if you are not settled in your heart about everything? What if you know that you are saved and not going to hell, which is good news, but you are not healed? What can you do to protect and take care of your mental health?

Emotional health has been a subject long talked about in any community. We are all aware of our feelings and how we feel about something, but when it comes to our mental health and mental strength, this topic is one we don't talk about a lot. For many of us, we live under a dark cloud that others cannot see because they are focused on other factors that make us seem "normal."

Some would say that there is nothing wrong with you; you are just lazy, unmotivated, or you want attention. They don't know your thoughts, your pain, and your frustration. It is in this silence that you keep moving, and you see the eyes, the judgments, and the snickers of people laughing at your pain. This is enough to make a person go insane, get mean, or think the worst.

The Bible says to think on things that are lovely, wonderful, good, and have a good rapport. But how many of us are thinking about these things? How many of us are looking at old photos and growing frustrated with the person we have become? How many of us are saying things will get better in time, no big deal? But we are falling deeper into a depression.

We stop caring about how we look, how we sound, and it is a struggle to get up and to lie down each day. We are searching for something to anchor our thoughts, to maintain our hope, but we are coming up empty. Some work can be done in silence, with reading books, prayer, and attending church services or group meetings. Then there are times when we need more than that.

Sometimes our wounds are so deep, and we are so locked in place, that we cannot pull out the energy to get to the next step. We can believe in God and want to go to heaven, even to give up on today, but this is not the Father's will for your life. He wants you with Him in heaven, yes, but He wants you to bring heaven here on earth, too. He needs you to fulfill your purpose before you go, and we shouldn't rush to leave. So, what do we do if we are struggling to be here?

I want to share with you something that I had to do in my life, and I encourage us all to do at some point. I had to seek out a counselor. I needed to go to someone who could understand where I was in life and take me by the hand to process my thoughts. We might not realize the areas we don't allow Yah to access in our lives. We can be so protective of our feelings, heart, or have a fear of judgment and correction, that we hide these parts from ourselves.

How can we surrender something we don't know is there? I didn't know I had several emotional traumas that impacted how I was living my life. I wrote a book series, Embrace Your Crown, that talks more about my journey to find and overcome heartbreak. I didn't want to write this book because as I wrote it, I felt the difference in how I was feeling. I noticed, probably halfway through the book, that the book wasn't just for the world, it was also for me!

I didn't realize why I had two marriages that failed. I didn't realize what those failures, or presumed failures, did to my heart and mental health. I blamed myself if I am honest. I didn't want to become a statistic. I hated the thought of raising my children as a single mother when I had been married and tried to do things right. I was frustrated that I couldn't seem to keep the pieces from falling down.

I didn't pay attention to the reason the marriages fell apart, before I had to deal with my heart on why they couldn't be faithful to me. What was so wrong with me that made them so unfulfilled, that going after women, or taking their ring off, was something I should grow to accept. I even thought about staying married on paper, living separately, not having a physical relationship, but a parenting and partnership. That, too, didn't work.

I tried to salvage the situation, but there was nothing left in my hands. Like running water, the ideas I had kept escaping my control and power. I took a year to gather my thoughts after the divorce. I tried to bury my interest in another relationship. For years, I feared what my life could be like if I got into another relationship. I felt a relationship was constricting. Not that I minded being guided, but I didn't like not completing a task that I knew was set before me.

I tried to postpone having a relationship until all of my tasks were completed, but love found a way to attract me when I least expected it. That wasn't the problem, but when I was willing to remove my boundaries to prove my love for someone else. I lost myself the more I tried to find myself in their arms. I knew it wasn't good, but I tried to pray it good, and make it good.

Have you ever tried to reverse what the Father has said about a person, only to come back to what He said after pain, divorce, heartbreak, shame, or guilt? No one likes these emotions; I, for one, don't. It broke my heart, and I didn't see it because I was still working. Still praying. Still hopeful, but I was broken.

I had to keep going for my children who needed me. I didn't mind the version they got of me, in the sense that I wasn't paying attention to how I looked, if they were good. I didn't care about who liked me or was attracted to me, because I already assumed no one would want a woman with four children. Today, I struggle with seeing how things can change sometimes for the better romantically with my time, and ironically, it bothers my children more than me for me to be single. I chuckle just thinking of their questions and counseling sessions to help me date again.

I have many friends who are older than me who have hopes to get married, to date, to start over, but they are where I was, and sometimes find myself. We can all feel like the future is bleak for marriage when we are looking and reliving the pain of our past. I had to shut off those thoughts so that I could appreciate the right person, at the right time, for all the right reasons.

Therapy is what helped me years ago to better my mind before my first marriage. I stood no chance at that time to be emotionally available for a serious institution like marriage. I was still hurting from the treatment of my stepfather and other forms of abuse I had suffered before. If I am honest, I was afraid of men. Yes, I was attracted to them, but I didn't know how to love them because perfect love casts out fear. I was very afraid in my relationships before I got my feet under me and my voice to have confidence in what I deserved.

I was used to providing excuses for others, but not for myself. I was understanding and I was willing to forgive others, but I struggled with giving that same grace to myself. I would say that anything that happened to me, good or bad, was because it was the Father's will, and I found a way to accept it as something designed for me. I didn't understand how to process my faith in relation to my life.

I was reading some scriptures out of context and thinking it justified staying in unbearable circumstances. I thought staying made me tough and proved I was committed to long-suffering for Christ. But I was only suffering in sin, because the Father did not get the glory from my sinning to be with someone that I wanted to get saved! I know it sounds crazy when we think sinning on one hand, will be overlooked, because our intention is to sin to bring someone to Christ.

This is not the way to witness. I essentially became like the sinner I was hoping to bring to the marvelous light. I now needed more light, Word, studying time, time in prayer, and for the Father to increase in me so that I decrease to function again in my life. For some of us, we became something we weren't intended to become to please someone or a situation, and now, we don't recognize ourselves. This is what can break you emotionally, too.

I had to surrender everything I wanted and thought I wanted to the will of God, and not desire my will for God for my life. There is a difference. Some of us are suffering because we have believed a lie so long that no one can pry it from our hearts and minds except Yah Himself! The truth is that the Father works through His Holy Spirit, the Word, and people. Some of us hear His Voice, but we silence it, saying that it is negative thoughts. Some of us read the Word and choose not to believe it. Some of us hear the Word of truth from others, or we are scared to seek out a therapist because we think we know what they would say.

Unless the Lord Builds the House
PSALM 127

A Song of Ascents. Of Solomon.

Unless the Lord builds the house,
  those who build it labor in vain.
Unless the Lord watches over the city,
  the watchman stays awake in vain.

2 It is in vain that you rise up early
  and go late to rest,
eating the bread of anxious toil;
  for he gives to his beloved sleep.

3 Behold, children are a heritage from the Lord,
  the fruit of the womb a reward.

4 Like arrows in the hand of a warrior
  are the children of one's youth.

5 Blessed is the man
  who fills his quiver with them!
He shall not be put to shame
  when he speaks with his enemies in the gate.

CREATOR OF PROGRAM:
KLE SERVICES

YOURLEGACYMOMENT.COM
855-864-1514
INFO●YOURLEGACYMOMENT.COM

There will be no transformation in your life nor a preservation of your legacy if you are not willing to align your life to the plan of Yah. You will perform your own will and your thoughts, our thoughts are lower. We can live our days in judgment of ourselves, and keep settling for situations beneath us. We can end up like the lady at the well who had a fifth husband, and even he didn't belong to her.

We want to be loved so badly, and it is because Yah is Love. We are meant to fill our lives with Him, the pure light, and this is what makes people happy and enables them to find joy in staying together through storms. That is the power of Love! If we have everything, but not charity or love, we have nothing. Everything we are building is in vain. I love what it says in Psalms 127 and verse 1, "Unless the Lord builds the house, those who build it labor in vain. Unless the Lord watches over the city, the watchman stays awake in vain."

A lot of us are busy working and giving our best, but how many of us are committed to the process of aligning our lives to the Father's will? How many of us think we cannot trust Him, when it is our emotions, thoughts, and actions that we cannot trust? Our hearts can betray us, or as I am writing it in a book, "We Lie Through Our Actions." It is not just about what we say, but what we do.

Author K. Lee
GET BOOKS BY ME! K . LEE

It's not just about saying I am good, but proving you are good with your actions. What do people do, how do they feel, how do they talk, that is the evidence of them being good? In 1 John, it tells us to examine ourselves many times to see if we are in the faith. We have to examine ourselves to see if we are emotionally healed or still leaking. Leaking pain and harboring pent-up emotions make our soul weak. We cannot think rationally, and we are prone to succumb to the spirit of anger or depression.

We will seed the spirit of jealousy, and can get jealous of others and either take that out on other people through anger, or self-sabotage because we are not what someone else says, don't have what they have, or can't do what they do. This is a mindset, though, because not everything you can do, say, or have is what they have either. When we have confidence in how the Father made us, we can learn to extend His love in every other aspect of our lives.

If you are struggling with managing your emotions, I want to let you know there is help. I know of a pastor, Dr. Bostic, who is just as committed to God, prayer, and using the Bible as a foundation for his life as he is sincere about helping people through therapy. I want to encourage you to connect with someone who can help you walk through emotional healing–why? Because it is important for you to preserve your life now and the one for your future.

Dr. Bostic & Dr. Martin
CONNECT WITH PROFESSIONALS

This book is about you living now and preserving the legacy you want to share for your future. If you are unsure of where to go from here or just want someone to talk to, pastor Dr. TC Martin is also a woman you can feel comfortable talking with about how you feel and what you are going through. If you are dealing with a long-term illness and the Father has not healed you, but you still want to love Him. You still need help processing this condition, or a condition of someone you love; she can help bring the loving hand you need to your life by being a living example.

I also want to provide a reading list for you to connect with powerful books written by me and others who I believe will bless your life.

You are doing great. Let's keep going. Only three short chapters to go. Remember to take advantage of all of the offers and bonuses in this book to help you transform your life! If you want to dive deeper, don't be afraid to invest in yourself or someone you love.

Release Pain - K Lee (Those battling Robbery, Injustice, Unfaithfulness, Betrayal, Jealousy, and Anger)

Embrace Your Crown Series - K Lee (Those who feel inadequate and are struggling to find balance in their life.)

From Pain to Purpose - Stephen Barbee (Those who have been addicted to drugs, alcohol, or served time in jail or prison, who want freedom from addiction and entrapment.)

Release the Honey Within You - Shantay Adams (For those who are overly aggressive and need to break the spirit of anger by finding value in themselves again.)

From Wounds to Wholeness - Kemi Itayemi (Those who are afraid to be alone but need to understand to get to wholeness, they won't have that in someone else, but need to find it first in themselves.)

Physical Health
HEALTH, NUTRITION, AND PHYSICAL HEALTH

It is a no-brainer to want to be healthy. To understand that taking care of your health is part of preserving your life and legacy. The way we treat our physical selves can be closely linked to how we feel emotionally and mentally. If you have not resolved or are not working to heal from pain or trauma in these areas, I highly encourage it. When we feel weak or are poor in physical health, it usually stems from other areas also being out of balance.

What are the things that show up in this part of our lives that can keep us bound? Unforgiveness. I know we have heard this word so much in the streets and the church, but unforgiveness will sow a seed in your life or in the lives of those you love that can make them implode. You can see people transition from a happy person to sad or angry. You can see them eat to hide their pain, and they refuse to talk about it.

They have chosen to latch on to food as a protection mechanism, and when people judge them for their weight, appearance, body odor, or something like that, they say you are not tolerant. You are cruel because you are pointing at the aftermath of their unresolved pain. Spirits don't like it when you call them out. People don't like it when you talk about their pain, like a wounded dog, they can snap back or be so weak they absorb the hit.

It is not okay to allow your physical body to suffer because you are emotionally or physically unwell. If you know you eat when you are sad. If you have a craving like a pregnant woman, and you are not carrying a child, or even if you are and you know you eat until your pants get tight. You have a problem that is deeper than you think.

Sometimes this is a learned behavior you adapt from trauma. Perhaps you grew up with not enough, so your body is accustomed to overeating to compensate for the times you unknowingly expect days of lack. When we feel low, we think, 'I'll treat myself to ice cream.' You go from eating it occasionally to eating it several times a week after meals. We start to pattern our lives around food. If we're going to an event, the first thing we consider is what kind of food will be available.

Some will say that is something people with a weight problem do, but it isn't, I assure you. Some of the binge eaters on YouTube and other platforms who gorge on food for the entertainment of others will pile down food and celebrate their gluttony. Gluttony is a sin. It is one of the deadly sins, to be exact, and it is for a reason. Your body wasn't meant to handle the diets we eat. We might think it's okay to eat a lot of foods that are terrible for us because we'll go to the gym and work it off.

But how do you work off a bioengineered ingredient? How can you release forever chemicals from your body that are in the foods you eat regularly? How are you going to purge the body of the foods you eat regularly if you don't practice a cleanse? I know cleansing out the body is something many of us don't want to talk about, but we should.

The body is filled with healthy bacteria. Your body knows how to clean itself and heal when its organs are functioning properly. But what if they are not functioning as designed? What if our organs become damaged, or they are weak because of a lack of nutrition–how do we overcome that? Some run to pills to fix their cravings. It is easier to pop a pill with a million side effects than to be accountable for our own health.

I want to talk about this subject because it impacts me, too! I know people look at those who appear to be skinny or large and make a judgment about who is healthy or unhealthy. I can tell you, it wasn't until I did the Daniel's fast for Lent one year that I largely reduced the amount of meat I saw as necessary in my diet. Here in America, we think meat should be a protein we have for every meal. We eat sausage at breakfast, a hamburger for lunch, and steak for dinner, and call that good eating.

The problem is, steak takes a week to digest. Pork has some forever chemicals and increases sodium in our bloodstreams. They say that pork is a free food to eat if you're diabetic, but that is a statement made without accounting for other factors impacting your health. Yes, pork may not increase your body's sugar levels, but it does increase your salt consumption. Pork, aka pig, are animals that don't have pores to sweat. So as they live outside in any condition, instead of them sweating from the sun, they roll in mud to cool off.

That sweat is what makes the meat naturally salty. This creature is also known for its eating habits. A pig will eat anything in front of it. Trash, animals, feed, and the list goes on and on. I have seen videos on social media, and you may have too, about how they are grinding up trash and turning it into feed to give to pigs. This is why you cannot trust everything you hear about what you should eat.

The last thing about a pig is that the bible calls it an unclean animal. It is unclean because of everything listed, and the Father said an animal with a split hoof is not fit for food consumption. Yes, a man with spiritual problems, demon possession, when the Messiah cast them out, they asked to go into the pigs. The pigs did jump off the cliff, so those pigs died all good there, but the animal is unclean and not what the Father wants us to eat.

During slavery, a physical prison, we were forcibly fed pork. We were left with scraps to survive. We essentially were spiritually compromised with swine, another word for pig, on purpose. At that time, there was nothing we could do about it because it was part of the judgment. Part of other people's choices and traditions were passed on to us. Now, as a leader in your family, what will be your choice concerning your health?

As time progresses, we should preserve recipes and things we learned, but we can also make them healthier and fit the times we live in. Fasting is something that was a tradition for the Hebrews. It is a tradition, even now, for some people not to eat at certain times of the day to help regulate their hunger, consumption, and overall health. Do you know that fasting for three days straight can help restart your body's systems?

There are many programs that can help you become healthy, which will suggest vitamins and other care as you fast. I understand that fasting isn't for everyone, but you have to ask the question, why? Is it because you don't want to? You can't picture yourself going a long period without food? You are undisciplined? Are the medications you have to take blocking your ability to fast? Or something else?

I understand that we all have different health factors affecting our lives. I remember that after I did the Daniel's fast, I was open to keeping fasting as part of my life. Sometimes it's not about eating nothing, but about choosing to eat better. I could only eat fruits and vegetables during the fast. I felt lighter, I didn't feel full, but I wasn't starving. I needed to correct my eating habits and work to control my appetite. So to up the ante in my health journey, I set out to do a 24-hour fast.

I wasn't sure that I could do it. I thought we had to have food, and I must eat. However, part of a fast is the spiritual element. We fast so that the physical voice in our bodies can be covered by our spiritual voice. We are killing the cares of the flesh, to be able to resurrect the power of the spirit in our lives. Fasting is how you connect more with the spiritual realm because you are opening yourself to be light and to hear.

In the first 24-hour fast, I did just fine. I remember praying to God and asking many questions. I was excited to read my devotional that day and write notes. I spent the day seeking God's face in different ways, and then I became intentional with sharing the Word I read with others to keep it in my memory. The more I kept pulling on the spirit, the more I realized it had to give me.

A 1-day fast turned into a 3-day fast. I didn't drink much water, if any, during this fast. I was shocked when I finished, because I had sworn I needed to eat every day. I did get the temporary headaches, which I think came from dehydration. So I do recommend drinking water now that I know better. Your body is also detoxing from the foods and cravings we have.

Many of us don't know, but your body can be trained to crave sugar and salt. These are the ingredients in food that can lead to an addiction. These two ingredients can be more addictive than street drugs in how your brain will trigger you need more of them. Sometimes when we fast, our bodies aren't craving food so much as it craves junk food to get its high on sugar and salt.

Consecration is another term that is in the fasting

wheelhouse when you intentionally stop doing something for a period of time, or period, to grow closer to God. If you want to connect with Him spiritually more, a physical sacrifice in the form of fasting will be necessary. When the Messiah had to face going to the cross, He fasted to pray about the outcome. When there was a problem in the land during the Old Testament of the Bible, the people were asked to fast.

Fasting is part of life when you are in a hard place. If things aren't making sense, and you need to hear from God. One of the artists I will never forget is Mary Proctor. She is a folk artist from Florida, and when she was living in a trailer, she and her family suffered a grave loss. When her family was in the trailer, it caught fire, and smoke filled the air. If I am not mistaken, she found the door to get out, but none of her other family members did.

Or she was not there, and none of her family could see past the smoke to find a door to get out in time, before they died of consuming too much smoke. It was a terrible accident. She was heartbroken to see all of their caskets at a funeral to bury her parents and other family members. She decided to go on a 30-day fast because she needed to hear from God. She needed healing. What the Father told her to do on the 30th day is how we all know her, who knows her art.

She said on the 30th day, she was told to tell her story and the story of her family through her art. She is an artist who uses mixed media to tell the stories of scripture, preserve prayers, and commemorate her family's legacy by drawing their lives on doors. The very element that led to the death of her family, she used as a doorway to reach the world. She used her pain, after she released it to Yah, to heal others who have experienced great loss.

Sometimes loss can have us abuse ourselves physically through cutting, belemia, and other forms of physical self-harm. You need to speak to someone about these actions. I know of children whose parents had to be contacted because their child in middle school had been cutting themselves with plastic knives. They said they were curious, but what happens when they get too curious and use a real knife?

Emotional pain and isolation can cause adults and children to think of ending their lives or put the pain in another spot for distraction. Speaking about your pain is important because it impacts every level of your life. Yes, eating well is important. Taking care of your body so that your overall health will be good. Brushing your teeth each day and visiting the dentist are also important.

Gum and oral health is one of the areas we are being attacked because many of us don't go until we have a problem. We won't go for cleanings, annual, or regular visits, because we think if I have no pain, I have no problem. Prevention is also important. What you eat and how you take care of your mouth are essential.

Other lifestyle choices we make, like what addictions we give way in to other than food, we need to assess. Drinking, smoking, and taking illegal drugs all impact the body and your growth. If you want to live long, you will want your organs to function as designed for as long as possible. These factors can cut your life short or reduce the quality of life you will have.

Lifestyle changes are important. You want to ask yourself: "How am I preserving my legacy with my health? Am I making choices to be here or disappear?" If you are smoking, you should see a dentist because your teeth and, most importantly, your gums, can be greatly impacted by smoking. We know your throat, lungs, and energy can be impacted as well. I know people who are suffering from oral problems because they won't stop smoking.

What led to smoking in the first place? Most people smoke to reduce stress or to create an environment where they can escape their reality. What is wrong with your reality, though? Do you think there could be power, life there, if you redirected this need for smoking to something more beneficial to you? There is a saying, "Everything is possible, but not all things are profitable." You can choose to live your life however you want, but is how you live your life profitable to you?

Something we cannot forget when talking about health is how to heal the body. You can change your diet, you can work fasting into your life, you can remove ingredients from what you cook or buy. You can also take supplements that help your body get nutrients you don't have in your food. Does this mean you can eat any and everything? No, but it means if you are eating well and can't get all the foods you need into your diet, a safe way to get them is through supplements.

Not all supplements are equal. Some are new, others have been around for years. I personally like Juice Plus for helping with overall health. It gives you the fruit and vegetables we are not eating on a regular basis through gummies and tablets. I started my oldest daughter on Juice Plus when she was young, then we got away from it. When I got older, I was reintroduced to it, and a person I recommend you look up is: Dr. James A Dail Sr.

Dr. Dale has been taking Juice Plus for over 30 years. He is a 70 plus year-old-man who made the news and broke records for his athletic ability. He ran on the treadmill for 7 hours straight. He helps people heal their bodies and find meal plans and nutritional balance to take care of and heal their bodies. If you need to reverse your health condition or want to acquire better health now to live your days ahead, reach out to him for help in creating your plan.

If you are interested in trying Juice Plus, use this QR to order:

Juice Plus
LEARN MORE & ORDER

Before we leave this chapter, I must talk about the gym. I know 60-year-olds, 70-year-olds, they get into the gym like clockwork. It's not about having a rock-star body, but about keeping their body moving so they don't have problems bending, sitting, or performing general tasks. Our bodies are conditioned to perform how we use them. As you slow down on how the body is being used, it becomes increasingly laborious to use the body over time.

I am not the best with getting to the gym, although I pay for a membership every month. I know the importance of it, and I try to incorporate home workouts and a training schedule that better fits my schedule. If you cannot make it to the gym or don't care to go, that's okay. I do encourage you to get an app, join a group, a dance class, or walk the streets outside, but do something to keep your body moving on a regular basis.

Walking daily can help bring back a healthier you, especially when combined with other healthy habits. I am not a doctor, but I seek only to share my experiences and how I am working to take care of my health so that I can live a longer and healthier life. All this work I am doing to build up my future and preserve my legacy, my dear reader, I had better be here to see it unless the Messiah comes back, right?!

So, a good rule of thumb, from what I have been told, is to try to work out at least 3 to 4 times a week. You can skip a day or two in between to keep the body alert. When you do anything too religiously, the impact will fade on the body. So switch up your workouts. Don't just do the same thing each day, and consider working out specific parts of the body on different days.

Make a leg day, arm day, core, etc, to help you manage recovery also.

There are products that help with recovery, but honestly, I don't use anything like that. Not to say there is something right or wrong about it. If that is something you research and find to be helpful, go for it if it makes you feel healthy and will not harm your overall health. Read the ingredients to be sure of what you are consuming. Also, be open to activities that can make working out fun. Play games weekly with friends to take the pressure off of working out three times a week.

Some activities you can do that can be fun are going to the park, playing tennis, or other sports like basketball. You can visit indoor gyms and pay nearly nothing to work out if money is a concern. Recreation centers vary by state, but most offer access to a gym with weights for $10 a month. To go swimming is often only a few dollars, so go splash in a pool for a bit and take a friend. Working out in water also helps with balance and brings resistance that can be enjoyable in training.

Discover what works for you in terms of eating, overall health, and exercise. Don't forget to take care of things like your skin, hair, nails, and ears. These are things we can overlook or only focus on dressing up. Don't be afraid to try organic lotions within your budget; pay attention to what chemicals are in your body products and laundry soaps. Examine the chemicals in your hair products and the shoes you wear on your feet. Comfortable shoes are important, and they can still be fashionable.

I know that tattoos are a thing, but educate yourself on these before you get them. Understand what the figure represents and how it can affect your life. So many people have foreign names, articles, and images they know nothing about tattoo on their bodies. The bible speaks about marking the flesh, and he doesn't condone it. But if you have it, you are here now. One piece of science I thought was interesting about tattoos, the scientist said that tattoos are linked to anxiety. The more tattoos a person has, the higher their anxiety.

This is a form of cutting, although it looks fashionable. It is a form of mutilation, and if this is what you choose to do to yourself, the question is, why? Some say to remember this or that, but why not put it in a book? Maybe I am too simple. I am the only child my mother has who does not have one out of her five children. So have this conversation with yourself and others you love. If you find that they are in pain, or you are, seek help to guide you through the healing journey.

You thought I was going to end this chapter without giving you some love? Nope! I want to give you a free video that will help walk you through how to release pain from your life. If you enjoy the video, consider ordering the book or e-book to deepen your experience. Psst, it works!

Release Pain
ACCESS THIS BOOK

Financial Health
INVESTMENTS, INSURANCE, AND FINANCIAL HEALTH

The money section is the part of this book that many either look forward to or dread. We all know that life is expensive, and in your passing, the bills don't stop. Building a legacy is work, some argue, blood, sweat, and tears. How do you make this work to your good? Where do you go from here if your finances aren't cutting it and you don't have thousands or hundreds in the bank?

If you are reading this book early in life, that is good. If you are reading this book for yourself or someone else who is later in life, there is hope and options. I know the concern many would have as we get older or about our loved ones, "How will I afford this funeral?" We may think of these specifics when the time comes, but I would suggest that it is too late. Many people are dying with no financial plan in place. Most people are living with no financial plan in place, and I want to share some resources I have picked up to help you.

I am not a financial advisor or an expert on investments and financial education. However, I have encountered financial advisors who are knowledgeable about this subject and are eager to help you! Shantay Adams helps people understand how money works, so you can learn how to invest. Yes, I want to get you a free conversation with her so she can show you what you can do right now to understand how your money is working for you.

Latoya Maddox is a financial advisor who is an expert on so many things related to money and finance. These women understand finance, and when I say understand it, they know how to properly save it, invest it, protect it, and grow it. Money has numerous uses, and for the average person, many of these applications are not well understood. We are focusing on making money and paying bills; we are not worried about everything else. Some of us don't know where our money goes each month because we are focused on getting through the month.

This chapter might be uncomfortable to start, but I think you would love the simple nature of this chapter. I wrote this book to make your life lighter, the conversations easy, but productive. So, what can you do to help protect and preserve your legacy through your finances? How can you get wealth, protect it, and ultimately share it with your family?

I would recommend starting with financial education or a financial advisor. A financial advisor will help you look at your financial picture. They will need to ask you a series of questions to best understand how much is coming in and how much is coming out. They are there to help you strategize on how to handle your money. I know in our own heads we think: "I know how to do that already." But what have you put in place that can help you retire? What have you put in place to help you go on vacations, buy a house, or live life now?

What protections have you made to keep more of your money when you need it most? A financial advisor's goal is to help you track where you are spending your money. When you see where you are spending your money, you can best understand yourself. Some of us are trauma spending. We are buying ourselves flowers so we don't feel left out on holidays. We are buying things we don't need to be trendy. We are buying things because we gotta take advantage of a sale, even though we don't need more of an item.

We can think we are bargain shoppers, but we can become money-wasters. When we have no clear budget or struggle to cut our budgets down as our life situations change, we find that we don't have the finances we need to move our lives forward in other areas. Some grandparents and parents who grew up with large families struggle with making smaller portions. They still shop and do things as if they have a village to feed, but they don't.

Some people love to cook, and they do it every day, no matter whether they need more food or not. They eat their leftovers for lunch, but there is still enough left for dinner and lunch for the next two nights, but they still cook. When we do this, we waste food. I know for me, I buy stuff I don't eat. I say I am going to eat salads all week, but I don't; and after one day, I am over it. I eat all kinds of stuff on the other days. I see myself throwing away money every week or month from food I let go to waste.

I am sure I am not the only one shopping in the store, buying on principles I am not ready to operate in. I want to eat better, but sometimes it is a struggle. I stopped buying GMO and bioengineered foods years ago, in large part, and buying fresh and such is expensive if you don't eat it. If we don't appreciate the value of what we have, we can think of eating out. If we don't put enough importance on our budget, we will continue to overspend out of convenience.

I realized sometimes all I need is a handful of nuts and berries from my trail mix, and I can go another hour or two without a meal. I started packing snacks to keep me from buying even healthy alternatives while I am out. When we are buying out of convenience, we can easily overspend hundreds over our budget. Another way we can spend a lot is by using cards and not cash.

When we are not seeing the money leave our hands or bank account, but get a bill each month, the numbers can be staggering. This is how we spend ourselves into debt, or at least how I did it. I wasn't paying attention to the pile up because I was focused on what I felt I needed for that day. As a business owner, we can think of these grand plans when we don't even have one person to buy from us yet. I had to learn to think big, but plan small, so I can take the proper steps to get there.

It takes work to get discipline in spending. It takes heart to tell people no, when they ask you to go somewhere or spend money you don't have. Holidays can be the worst. During these big holidays when everyone else is spending, you may feel the pressure to spend too. You might think: "Let me live a little," but that means you pay a lot. Don't get sucked into this guilt trip of having to spend money to keep others happy. Picking up the bill all the time, even if you can afford it, if it overextends your budget, stop it.

During your conversation, a financial professional will ask you questions about your assets and liabilities. What do you have that you can pull value from, and what are you paying for that you can't make an asset? We don't always see how what we spend should give back to us like we give to it. I started this principle in my life years ago, and I try not to spend money on things that don't give back to me. If I buy a new phone, I look at the bill and say, "What will pay for this bill?"

Will this phone give me more clients? Make me more money? Make me more efficient? Increase my time or productivity? If the answer is something that I don't value, like it will get people off of my back. I don't buy it. I had a phone for many years, actually until it broke. I had another phone that I didn't update until my son put it into the toilet. He was two and I said, "I ain't buying another phone like this until and if I need it."

I got the phone initially to call clients in other countries and not pay absurd amounts of money. Technology has come a long way, and there are other platforms that enable you to communicate without international calling. I hardly ever buy anything because I am tired of something else. I buy stuff I need to make my life easier after I have struggled enough with something inferior first, and the demand is there.

I go to a lot of shows with my books. We have to use these bins that have wheels, but the wheels bang into our legs as we walk. I thought having wheels on the bins would eliminate the need to carry them, but it didn't. So, to save our calf muscles, I bought a new heavy-duty wagon. Additionally, I work several shows a month and plan book tours that will cover the costs of both the bins and the wagon in one show.

I use this same principle with my children. When they ask me to buy stuff, I reply with, "Why?" They are not taken aback anymore when I ask. They tell me their reason, and if it doesn't line up with my priorities, it is not purchased. "Because I want it" is not sufficient. My oldest son always wants three things in the store, no matter the store. So I have mastered the "no," because I know he will ask for something else before we exit the store. Yes, many times he leaves with nothing other than what I went in there for.

If you rent or buy will be a question. Some people feel like renting is throwing your money away. I get that, but some people don't buy for many reasons. If they can live for cheaper than a mortgage elsewhere, they do. If they can skip out on repair costs and other factors homeowners have to worry about, they do. Or if they want to be free to move around when they want, not owning a house keeps them free as a bird.

I also understand why buying a house makes sense. You can have an asset that increases in value that you can later live off of. You can have a fixed place that is stable in your life. You can have a home that builds memories, more space, land, and have pride of ownership. There are other financial benefits to owning a home, too.

You can buy and sell real estate to build up your net worth because real estate is an industry that may cycle, but it will always increase over time if you can hold on to it and sell if you must at the right time. I bought a house a few times, and all my experiences weren't good. One time, I bought a house, and the damage was covered under my policy. However, the insurance company found a way not to pay for the damage to my property, to my stuff that was ruined, and they dropped me from my policy.

I hate to think what people would do if they were dropped from a policy, like during the wildfires on the West Coast, because insurance companies didn't want to pay. We hear of other horror stories where wear and tear isn't an insurance claim but a homeowner's problem. These sneaky bills may be why some of us are hesitant to make a purchase. I would say to speak to a financial planner about what is best for you and your goals. Renting or buying can help you get to your goals, depending on where you are and what you want to accomplish.

I know that some of us don't buy because we can't.

Some of us can't rent properly because of the same reason, our credit. Credit in this country is important, and not understanding your money is the fastest way to ruin your credit. When your credit is ruined, we know how difficult it can be to find your way into a home, a rental, and even some jobs. There are solutions out here to help you if you need to clean up your report or get a second chance with credit. Bankruptcy has a purpose, and some people may need to seek out a lawyer to get that kind of help.

What I would like to share is my journey with credit repair. I had some things on my report, mostly late payments, and a few small bills. Some of the bills I didn't pay on principle because I didn't owe the money. I had a company that billed me for another month, when I had already canceled the service and had proof of it. Their excuse was, "Well, we see that, but you still owe it." So I ignored the bill and let it hit my credit report in my ignorance.

It was little things like this that were bringing my score down. Something as simple as having your name correct on all pages can help you score points, too. There are many things you can do, can contest, to improve your credit scores. There are ways to get the benefits similar to bankruptcy without filing. Credit repair is not the same thing as bankruptcy, but it can help you with a fresh start. I do recommend speaking with a specialist to get all the details.

A company I used for credit repair that costs me less than a $1,000 was 24/8 Solutions. They helped not only me, but my mother, who had student loan debt on her report. She had tens of thousands of dollars in debt. This has always stopped her from buying and evictions in her far distant pass, kept her from renting. He was able to remove those debts, or hide them from her report legally, with a process that helped my mother buy her first house!

24/8 Solutions
ACCESS THIS FREE RESOURCE

At the age of nearly 60, she bought her first home. It can take time to buy a house, but don't give up on the dream if that is your goal. A financial planner or advisor can help you organize your savings, a credit repair specialist can help you clean up your credit, and a banker can help you get financed and find programs to afford your house with money back.

There are benefits to buying a home, and what it does for your soul, heart, and mind is valuable too. Having a place where people can return to no matter their life's course is a valuable resource. I know insurance is meant to protect your family in times of need. We have health insurance, which helps to offset larger expenses. Not having insurance is one of the worst decisions we can make, as it can result in higher costs when we don't have it to pay.

For my life, I had to get several types of insurance.

I needed health insurance, life insurance, renters insurance, and even business insurance. I also got gap insurance on my car in addition to driving insurance. I believe in the principles of insurance and why we should have it. Did you know the reason why banks made so much money during slavery was because the colonizers insured their cargo, the human lives they stole.

If people died on the boat, they collected on their premiums. If they lived, the banks got richer because no payout was due. Insurance is a business for sure, and I suggest connecting with licensed agents to help you select the right kind of insurance you need. With my experience of hiring a health insurance company I had never heard about and them not paying on not one of my claims, I learned the hard lesson of not trusting new and emerging companies without proof of their business ethic.

I will never buy insurance again blindly without looking further into the company's history. I suggest having a lawyer to help you read your policy and make sure you understand it and agree to the services early on. I do recommend having Legal Shield to help you with this, and Rebecca Triggs is my agent of choice.

Rebecca Triggs
LEGAL SHIELD

I know companies you've never heard of can be

cheaper, but can you trust their policy? Will they pay out? Are they a scam or a company that will discontinue your plan once claims come in? Yes, going with a reputable company could mean spending a few dollars more each month. But I would rather spend those few dollars more if that means I have a solid plan that I can believe will be there in my time of need. Life insurance is a policy you want to do your research on and pick a company worth the money you invest. Also, picking the right plan for the coverage you want.

For life insurance, I had heard of the topic when I was younger, but I didn't think long enough to buy it. I thought I couldn't afford it. I was on the fence about what kind of insurance I should have, term or whole life. I spoke with my Life Insurance Agent, Yulanda Dyer, and she helped me to understand the two and build a plan that was within my budget.

Yulanda Dyer
YOUR INSURANCE PROVIDER

For children, you can get a plan for like $20 or 30 bucks a month. I thought, "Man, that is cheaper than the cost of getting them a phone and will last longer." By the time they are 40 years old, they will have over 100k accessible to them with interest to do whatever they need. So I am not worried about them buying a house, getting married, and things like that, because the policy will pay for it. I want to double the numbers, too, so they can have money to start a business and live if they need the help.

Protecting your children and giving them something doesn't have to be when you die, or somebody dies; it can be for as long as you both live. I don't want the pressure of buying them a car financed, I want to buy the car cash and negotiate. I want to have options, and not be forced to spend 3 or 4 times the value of something just to obtain it. I want to be smart about money so I can keep more of it and reinvest it.

Saving money is not the best way to have money, but through investing, you grow money. Life insurance can be seen as an investment policy if you select the right one for your situation. Again, I am not an agent, and I am only sharing my experience. I spend less than $140 a month to cover myself and my four children. We all will have nearly a million dollars if I keep maintaining and nurturing the account payouts, and if I were to die under certain conditions, we would have nearly 2 million dollars.

Tell me what family could not use a million dollars or two? You don't have to buy a house solely to have money; you can also get other assets to build toward your goal. So there is hope for renters, and everyone to better their finances based on their goals and needs. Lastly, you need a will and a living will. This document will help to allocate your assets and responsibilities, and give you confidence that your final rights will be honored. It can keep your finances from being subject to legal arguments and going into probate court.

I suggested that you take advantage of the free offer resource in this book, but also, meet with a lawyer to protect your assets and look into getting a trust. Trust protects assets and can help you transfer your wealth to your children and family without fees. Latoya Maddox knows this process and has helped save many people from financial ruin. Ask a financial planner how this works and what other benefits you can take advantage of.

TELL YOUR STORY, ACHIEVE YOUR DREAMS, PRESERVE YOUR LEGACY

Now we get to the meat and potatoes: How do we bring all these categories into how you will preserve your legacy? As an author, publisher, and ghostwriter, I can tell you that telling your story in your own words brings a reward to your soul that cannot be easily put in words. When you can write your life down, read it, and share it with those you love, there is power in it.

I help people every day to write their stories and publish books. I love editing and seeing the finished products. One thing I realized was how many of my family members I didn't know their stories. We can easily look at the success of someone, but if we don't understand the how, how are we going to duplicate it?

It breaks my heart when family members pass and no one gets a recipe, learned a trade secret, or their own heritage, because we were too busy or didn't write down what we were told. Our memories can fade over time, and we can lose pictures in a fire or flood. So, what can we do to preserve our legacy, and why is it important?

So far, I have talked about preserving your legacy through your spiritual and emotional health, mental health, physical health, and financial health. Now I want to show you how to preserve your story and how to keep your voice healthy so that your children, grand-children, and great-grandchildren know it. They will know of your struggles and the moments when you overcame them. They can see how they too act like you or look like you as they go through your pictures.

Do you know that telling a story is the only way to increase the chances that your children won't repeat your story? When we are brave enough to examine our history and learn from it, we can share these valuable lessons with our family and even other families. We can be a voice that impacts nations. Most people in the bible never thought they would have stories we still read today, but God did!

We all are experiencing the goodness of Yah and his gifts to us, so why should we die only knowing it for ourselves? Why not share your story with your children, regardless of whether they want to listen now or later? When you are dead and gone, that is when your voice sometimes becomes the strongest; however, it often fades because it relies on memory.

How many will forget something you said, or things that happened? If you want to preserve your legacy, you have to preserve your story. You have to preserve your voice. In preserving your story, I have three suggestions that I recommend, and all of them have a corresponding resource you can use.

The first: You have to tell your story. To tell your story, you can record it and save it as audio. You can record it on video, and you can record it in a book. If you want to make sure your voice doesn't get lost, you want to record it and write it down. You also need to keep it in a safe place, so when people want to come back to it, it is there.

Can you imagine the impact we would have if we had video or even audio to go with the bible illustrations we read? To have a personal account from David and others telling their story from their own mouth? I think there is tremendous value in it, and with technology, it can be done.

Video Production: Interview

LEARN MORE ABOUT THIS RESOURCE

Second: Achieve your Dreams. Don't be afraid to dream and live your dreams, no matter your age. Yes, you may have to operate with a level of caution. Yes, you will need faith and hope. Yes, there is room for both of them to exist. You don't have to have it all figured out. I have a guide that can help you start a business and even publish a book, if those are things you want to do.

Sometimes knowing the road ahead makes the journey lighter. Don't neglect yourself and bring your greatest gifts to the grave; share them now. It's not too late if you are breathing. You can also choose to invest in someone who can be your hands and feet, who has a like mind or vision as yours. But be part of the story, and make that part of your story. It makes life worth living.

Third: consider the plans you want implemented for your end-of-life ceremony. I know from experience it is a difficult time to ask family who are still mourning your departure, to pick your casket, move your body, deal with the morgue, flowers, brochures, ceremony details, pictures for the wake, video elements, and the list goes on and on right after a loved one dies. I remember when my niece passed away, how difficult it was for my sister to be present and to make these decisions when she was still trying to accept that her daughter was gone.

It is a moment in my life that I would have loved to step up for her and other families who are in mourning, and thinking about these questions is just too much, too soon. At the core of "Your Legacy Moment" is the message of protecting your voice, telling your story, and offering support to your family during their time of loss.

What I offer you with this book are free resources that anyone can use, regardless of their budget, to get their affairs in order for the time they live and for their passing. I have met people whose children passed away

Congratulations

For wanting to take your dream of owning your business to the next level! Turn Keys Solution is your guide for creating your Mission, Vision, Client Avatar, and Sales Structure. If you have that nailed, then you might need help with Sales and Automating your business with helpful tools like a CRM and More.

Turn Key Solution can help you:

Select Your Process

- Create your Vision
- Mission Statement
- Brand
- Tagline
- Client Avatar
- Define Your Sales Cycle
- Sales Structure
- Content Creation
- Marketing
- Promotion
- Event
- Nailing Your Pitch
- Elevator Pitch
- Public Speaking
- Sales Tips
- CRM
- Email Campaigns
- Digital Numbers
- Website Development
- Social Media & More

KLETURNKEY.COM

Let's launch your business right!

Complimentary
CONSULTATION

Congratulations!

You have taken a great step forward to get your book, ebook, audiobook, or script completed, and I commend you. The best way to complete your book or script is with WAE Process!

WAE Process can help you:

- Write Your Life Story
- Write Your Novel
- Write Your Screenplay or Theater Play
- Format Your Book
- Format Your Ebook
- Format Your Audiobook
- Format Screenplay or Playwright (Theater)
- Publish Your Book
- Publish Your Ebook
- Publish Your Audiobook
- Design Your Cover
- Create Characters
- Copyright Books, Audiobooks, and E-books
- Register Scripts and Plays with Writing Guilds and Copyright
- Academic Writing

Reach 44k outlets around the world like Amazon, Barnes & Noble, and thousands more!

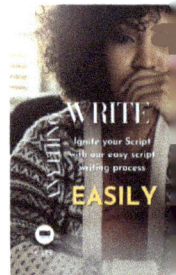

Complimentary
CONSULTATION

Select Your Process

from unexpected circumstances. Gun violence claims the lives of many children every day in this country. Having a policy on children is essential. I learned from my niece passing away at 16, and being diagnosed at 3 years old as a type 1 diabetic, that the sooner you get a policy, the better.

Sometimes we don't get sick as we get older, but we can have our battles start as children. When you purchase a life insurance policy for children, it can remain with them even if they develop issues later that would prevent them from obtaining a new policy. I recommend that you all look into insurance and other benefits mentioned in this book.

"I wanted to ensure that I provided you with nearly $5,000 of value in this book, and now I want to double that value to $10,000!"

I know for some of us, we might not care if the world hears our story, but we want our loved ones to know us. We want them to have our story accessible to pass down at any time, and any year, and have it in a central place that can be accessible. Some of us might be intimidated by the process of writing down our story and putting it into a book. I understand being a published author of nearly 50 books at the time I am writing this book, my 47th book!

I don't want you to feel overwhelmed with telling your story, and I want to make it easy for you to write it down in your own voice so you can preserve your story for your children and grandchildren. This is great for families who are close and even better for those who have not been close, were adopted, or gave up children through adoption, or you might have fallen out with family that you would like to sort out the issue.

In your book, you can include your story, personal letters to family members, last words, pictures, and even links to other things you want to share about your life or thoughts. Books are something that will outlast a life because they can be reprinted if there is ever a fire or an unforeseen act of God. You don't have to worry about only one person having the pictures, when everyone can have them if they have the book!

This is the easiest way to share information about your life, and with this book, I offer you a service that would cost over $4,500 to complete for less than half of that price. This legacy offer is less than WAE Process service fees with discounts!

What I will help you to do with the Legacy Plan is: Plan your book. When we plan the book, our team will outline the chapters, questions, and suggest elements for your book based on your initial interview. We will take pictures from you to include in your book. We will design the book's interior and exterior pages, which include the cover. We will edit the book and set it up with the printer. If you decide later to publish the book and make it available to the world, for an additional fee, we can help you do that, too! Lastly, you will get free copies of the book and can reorder as many as you like by contacting us to place your order.

Another option we offer is to make your audio files and video accessible to your family. If you choose to film your interview, we can film it for you, edit the video and audio, and provide you with the files. The best part of this is that we can store the files on a platform that makes them accessible for years to come.

It is one thing to read the book, but to hear your voice and see your face, what child wouldn't love to have that? We can take care of getting this done for you and also help you plan your end-of-life service, where we will manage your service on your behalf. We will implement your request and make sure your family has separation and time to grieve during this difficult time. We can arrange for a chaplain to be available for the family and have them present during the wake and the service.

Having someone to claim the body shouldn't have to be your loved one's task, we feel. We want to help you organize your program, write your obituary, have an original poem written by me (Author K Lee) or a published author write an original poem for you, design your graphics for your printed program, write down your preferences for casket, flowers, colors, and the venue for the service and wake.

Having these items picked out doesn't hasten death; it prepares for it when the time comes.

In closing, I would love to help you by giving you over $10,000 in services if you choose to take advantage of all of our offers, or $5,000 if you desire to access our free benefits. We want to ensure you have what you need to preserve your Legacy. To take full advantage of these offers, I would like for you to book a consulta-

Your Legacy Moment.com
855-864-1514
KLE SERVICES

LEGACY SERVICES

- Program Creation & Design, Obituary Writing, Original Poem for the departed, Song Play List Creation, Picture Collage

- Logistical and Chaplaincy Support for your Family for handling calls and your request for burial, flower arrangements, venues, wake, funeral home communication, and homegoing service. We will also film your interview and edit the video to share with your family during the service or whenever you'd like to share it.

- Lastly, we can help you write, edit, and print your life story to share with family. If you want to publish it, you can do that, too!

tion with us to help discuss what you have an interest in, and how we can help you plan for your future. You don't have to purchase anything to get:

I want to congratulate you on completing this book, and if you want to reach out to the individuals we spoke about in this book to get the help you need, scan the QR or give us a call. We will connect you with the proper people and get you the free offers in this book. I'm glad you're taking the next step, and you deserve to receive some rewards for doing the right thing. If you find local help to connect the dots, that is fine as well. This book is to show you there are paid and free resources to help you live better and protect your legacy for one day when you are gone.

It is a blessing to live to a ripe old age. It is a blessing to have ever existed, no matter how long or short a time. Enjoy being wonderfully and fearfully made for a time such as this. Lastly, I leave you with this inspiring poem, and original poem from me, your soul author, K. Lee.

Shalom, peace and blessings.

PEOPLE SAY WE SHOULD CARE ABOUT THE PAST.
THEY SAY WE SHOULDN'T LIVE SO FAST.
THEY SAY TO SPEND TIME WITH THE OLD.
BECAUSE THEIR STORIES HELP YOU TO BE BOLD.
BUT WE ARE BUSY TRYING TO FIND OUR WAY.
HISTORY WILL REPEAT, AND THERE IS NO ESCAPE.
IF YOU DON'T VALUE THE OLD, NO ONE WILL KNOW THE WAY FORWARD.
WE ARE MORE THAN THE MONEY WE MAKE.
WE HAVE HOPES, DREAMS, AND MISTAKES.
INSTANCES PEOPLE CAN LEARN FROM, HEROES WHO HAVE THEIR OWN SONG.
WHY WON'T YOU SPEND A LITTLE TIME TO SHARE YOUR STORY?
INVEST IN YOUR FUTURE FOR THE KING'S GLORY.
HE MADE YOU WONDERFUL AND GAVE YOU DAUGHTERS AND SONS.
HE WANTS YOU TO BUILD TRADITION, ROOTED IN HIM AND NOT GREED OR JEALOUSY.
WHEN WE CAN SEE THE TALENT IN OURSELVES, WE HAVE NO PROBLEM WITH BEING THERE.
WHEN WE KNOW THAT WE ALL HAVE SOMETHING TO SHARE, TO GIVE, WE ARE ABLE TO LIVE.
I WANT TO PLEAD WITH YOU, DON'T LET THE SUN GO DOWN AND YOU DON'T PRESERVE YOUR LEGACY.
STOP GROWING ENVIOUS OF THOSE WHO BUILT SECURITY.
BE A GOOD STEWARD, WHO GOT INSURANCE, BURYING IS NO LONGER A WEIGHT.
DEATH CAN BE SEEN AS PART OF LIFE AND A GREAT ESCAPE.
TO BE ABSENT FROM THE BODY AND PRESENT WITH GOD, WHERE IS HIS MISTAKE?
HE LOVES US AND WILL ALLOW US TO BLOSSOM AND FLOWER.
THEN AT THE RIGHT TIME, WE WILL BLOOM NO MORE, AND OUR LIVES WILL HIT THE FLOOR.
HOW YOU LIVE DOES MATTER.
HOW YOU EXPIRE MATTERS.
LIVE A LIFE WORTH LIVING, SHARE WITH YOUR CHILDREN AND THE WORLD WHAT THEY MUST KNOW.
TELL YOUR STORY, PRESERVE YOUR STORY.
SPEND THE TIME TO TALK ABOUT FAMILY AND GO TO REUNIONS.
GATHER, AND DON'T SKIP ASSEMBLING.
YOUR POWER IS IN YOUR EXPERIENCES AND UNDERSTANDING THE ROOT OF ALL OF THIS.
A SEED WILL GROW INTO A TREE.
THE TREE NEEDS THE SEEDS TO REPEAT.
LOVE EACH OTHER, FORGIVE EACH OTHER.
ENJOY LIFE AND LIVE.

About the Author
K . LEE

"God blesses those who work for peace, for they will be called the children of Yah (God)." Matthew 5:9

Dr. Lee has authored over thirty books across more than seven genres: adult, children, youth fiction, self-help, spiritual growth, novels, business, empowerment, etc. to help people in their most profound times of need.

She is also passionate about coaching programs and web courses she created for WAE (Write Anything Easily) Process, Embrace Your Crown, Turn Key Solution for Small and New Businesses, Transform Go Beyond Change (Personal Development, and The Lesson for youth and teenagers.
Connect and Shop my books:

AuthorKLee.com

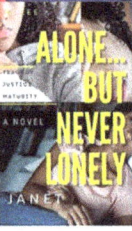

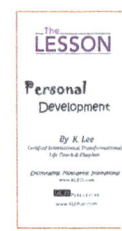

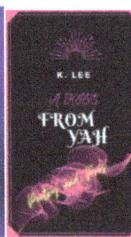

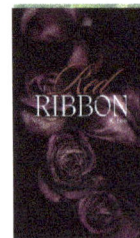

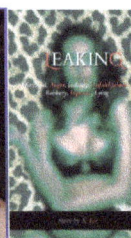

AuthorKLee.com Creator of *WAE Proce*

Explore over seven different book genres, and find something suitable for every member of the family.

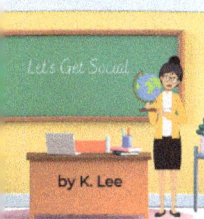

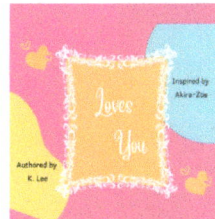

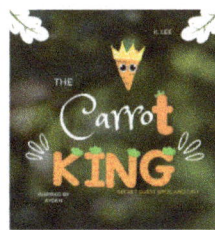

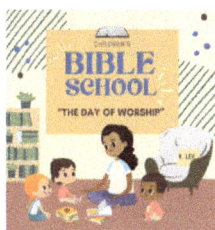

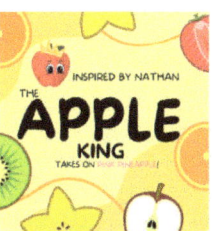

THE PLANT ...

SPARKLE'S SWEET GOOD-BYE
Akira-Zoe
& K. Lee

Samantha's GREATEST GIFT!
Kayda F.
K. Lee

KAYDA-BUG

Let's Get Social
by K. Lee

Loves You
Inspired by Akira-Zoe
Authored by K. Lee

Because I'm a Gentleman

the LESSON
Personal Development
By K. Lee
Certified International Transformational Life Coach & Chaplain

THE OLD MAN SAM AND HIS CAT

THE Carrot KING

CHILDREN'S BIBLE SCHOOL
"THE DAY OF WORSHIP"

the LESSON
Blended Families
By K. Lee
Certified International Transformational Life Coach & Chaplain

WITH NATHAN CS

123 with AYDEN

WHY YOU GOT an F

DON'T MY YUM

ARE YOU ... Sleepy, Baby?

INSPIRED BY NATHAN
THE APPLE KING
TAKES ON ...

Ugly SWAN

DANCING MOON
K. Lee & Ayden

Explore and learn more about published authors affiliated with KLE.

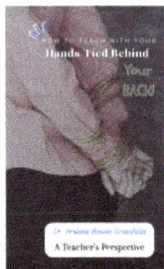

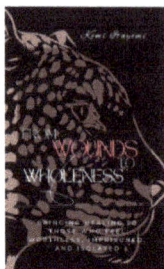

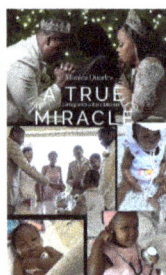

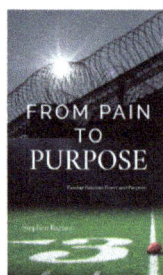

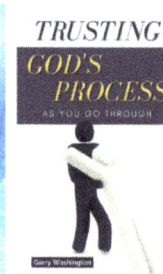

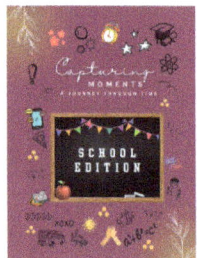
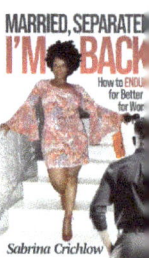

KLEPub.com

SCAN ME

Call or Text:

770-240-0089 Press Extension 1

Web: KLEpub.com

Email Services@klepub.com

It's time to start and finish **YOUR Story**!

KLE Publishing specializes in helping people become authors. In as little as 15 to 90 days, we can help you develop your books and e-books and publish to 39,000 outlets! We also offer audiobook services.

Write, Edit, Format, Publish
We can help from
Start to Finish.

www.ingramcontent.com/pod-product-compliance
Lightning Source LLC
Chambersburg PA
CBHW052120030426
42335CB00025B/3065